CASTLES OF THE LOIRE

PLACES AND HISTORY

Text
Milena Ercole Pozzoli

Editing Supervision by
Valeria Manferto De Fabianis

Art Director
Patrizia Balocco

Graphic Supervision by
Anna Galliani
Alberto Bertolazzi

Translation by
A.B.A.

1 The salamander, coat-of-arms of king Francis I, is engraved on the fireplaces of nearly all the castles in the Loire where the king resided.

2-3-4-5-6-7 Chaumont Castle was rebuilt between the 15th and 16th centuries on a hill that overlooks the village of the same name. Its "gentle" appearance typical of the Renaissance fashion, with its unmistakable conical roof, softens the heavy fortress-style structure.

© 1996 White Star S.r.l.
Via Sassone, 22/24
13100 Vercelli, Italy

Published in 1997 and distributed in the U.S. by Stewart, Tabori & Chang, a division of U.S. Media Holdings, Inc.
575 Broadway, NY, NY 10012
Distributed in Canada by General Publishing Ltd., 30 Lesmill Rd, Don Mills, Ontario, Canada M3B 2T6

Library of Congress
Catalog Card Number: 96-70320

ISBN: 1-55670-540-9

Printed in Italy by Grafedit, Bergamo.
Color separations by Graphic Service, Milan.
10 9 8 7 6 5 4 3 2 1

CASTLES OF THE LOIRE

PLACES AND HISTORY

STEWART, TABORI & CHANG
NEW YORK

CONTENTS

*F*rom Giens to Angers, by the calm waters of what has been called the loveliest river in France and along its major tributaries, hundreds of fortresses and castles appear as if by magic from the woods. But why should there be so many princely residences in this area?

One tragic night 600 years ago, the Burgundians put Paris to fire and sword. Tanguy du Châtel, a faithful servant of King Charles VI, hastened to the palace and, with a group of horsemen, escorted the 15-year-old dauphin of France to safety at Chinon Castle. Thus, on the night of May 28, 1418, began the history of the castles of the Loire. For a century the court of the kings of France, with their

8 top The walls of Chaumont Castle, shrouded in the morning mist, conceal a multitude of secrets and mysteries.

8-9 Chambord Castle, so grandiose as to seem almost unreal, looms up in the distance like a mirage.

9 Shooting parties take place every year in the huge grounds of Cheverny Castle, and the pack of dogs are exercised along the paths of the park under the guidance of a trainer every day.

retinue of noblemen and dignitaries, moved to the banks of the river. The dauphin (who ascended to the throne as Charles VII) and his successors found the Loire Valley to be the ideal refuge from the threats of a turbulent, unsafe capital. Great castles were built, ancient city walls restored and patrician residences erected, housing a wealth of splendors, intrigues, vendettas, courtly pageants and decadent love affairs.

10-11 Chambord
Castle ends the saga
of the Loire Valley.
Bristling with
pinnacles and
turrets, containing
endless halls and

chambers, the castle,
built on the banks of
the magical river,
was a king's last
dream, intended by
Francis I to evoke an
entire age.

11 top Starting from
the northwestern side,
the Chapel Tower is
followed by the west
wing of the galleries
(top right), the
Dieudonné Tower, the
Francis I Tower, the
east wing of the
galleries and the
Robert de Parme
Tower.

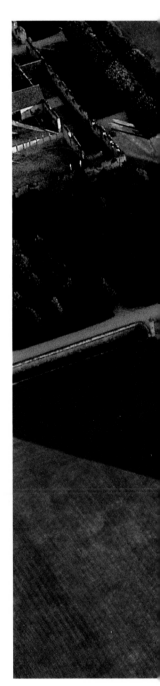

But in a letter written on his return from Madrid on March 15, 1528, Francis I manifested the desire to return "to sojourn in the good city of Paris." The Loire had lost the privilege of being the Valley of Kings. When the court left, the noblemen who had built princely residences, no less magnificent than the royal castles, left too. Thus the lights went out on that enchanted world that, centuries later, still evokes a dreamlike fascination. Princes and kings, courtiers and minstrels, queens and dukes still seem to tread that great stage. An invisible hand holds the strings of their memories. From the time of Louis XI to the present day, it has been said, the centuries have never obscured the fame of this garden, where François Rabelais plucked the roses of life. A million tourists visit it every year not only because of the castles, but also for the countryside, the cuisine, and the secrets held by a region that always has something to say. The villages, with their quiet squares basking in the sun, encircle the larger towns, where the living heart of the Loire beats. Through its markets, riverside restaurants and souvenir shops, to the backdrops of its better known castles, the history of the Loire is recounted in "sound and light." Every stone tells a story, every garden bears witness to the idle pleasures of a king, and every drawing room rings with the echoes of a bygone world. But the Loire Valley is only the main artery of a much larger green heart, also studded with castles steeped in history; the whole region is just waiting to be discovered, by traveling from castle to castle like a courtly minstrel. There are the more famous ones, perched on its banks or nestled in the woods: Chambord, Chenonceau, Blois, Amboise, Azay-le-Rideau, Langeais, Chinon, and so on. To the south, in the ancient land of Berry, there are the more defensive castles designed as military outposts, like the fortress of Culan, Meillant Castle, shrouded in the green mantle of the forest of the same name, and the castle of Ainay-le-Vieil. And there are the lesser known castles to the north, behind the Loire, such as Châteaudun, perched on a steep crag, Montigny-le-Gannelon, with its magnificent furnishings, Maintenon, still as it was when Louis XIV's secret wife lived there and, just outside Paris, Anet Castle, the little kingdom of Diane de Poitiers, mistress of King Henry II, which brings to an end the romantic and dissolute history of the Loire Valley castles.

14-15 The village of Chenonceaux, about 19 miles from Tours, is famous for the castle of almost the same name (Chenonceau without the "x"), built in the early 16th century for Thomas Bohier, tax collector under Charles VIII, Louis XII and Francis I.

16-17 The castle of Sully-sur-Loire, which has the tallest slate roof in the Loire Valley, stands like an island of pale stone suspended over the water.

The Castle of Sully-sur-Loire

Chambord Castle

Valençay Castle

Ussé Castle

Azay-le-Rideau Castle

Amboise Castle

Anel

Collines
du Perche

Maintenon

Eure

Chartres

Châteaudun

Montigny-le-Gannelon

Orléans

Montargis

Loire

Talcy

Sully

Gien

Loir

Chambord

Blois

Beauregard

La Verrerie

Angers

Chaumont

Cheverny

Tours

Amboise

Langeais

Villandry

Chenonceaux

Cher

La Chapelle d'Angillon

Ussé

Saumur

Azay-le-Rideau

Valençay

Maupas

Chinon

Loches

Monts du Morvan

Bourges

Bouges

Indre

Châteauroux

Meillant

Argenton

La Châtre

Ainay-le-Vieil

THE GENTLE SOUTHERN COUNTRYSIDE

18 top left The fortress of Culan, standing high on a crag, overlooks the Arnon River.

18 center left The perfect French-style garden of Bouges Castle, a linear square of pale Touraine stone with a classical beauty; the castle has no pinnacles or Renaissance influences.

At the southernmost border of the central Val de Loire region, before the architectural grandeur of the famous valley begins, the department of Cher has constructed the historical Jacques Coeur route, which leads to villages and castles. These castles were the theater of war centuries ago, when the area, which forms part of the ancient region once called Berry, divided the possessions of the king of France from those of the king of England. Visitors can still admire these outposts of bygone deeds, long roads and unusual itineraries entwining with the great river, until reaching Bouges Castle—with its precious furnishings—and Valençay Castle—residence of statesman Talleyrand—bring them back to the charm of castles that have never known war. In Culan, the 12th-century stronghold standing high on a spur of rock has the austere features of one who has known the hardships of sieges. It is an awe-inspiring fortress, with mighty round towers overlooking the Arnon. The great 15th-century fireplaces, two precious paintings attributed to Caravaggio, the original windows and precious historical relics testify to its past splendors. Its grandeur was due to the feats of Louis de Culan, admiral of France, who fought all over the world and was Joan of Arc's comrade in arms at Patay and Orléans. Famous personalities and leading statesmen have stayed at the grandiose castle, last but not least being General de Gaulle in November 1951. Indre, which borders on Cher, is another department whose treasures are worth a visit. The most romantic is the magnificent country home of George Sand at Nohant, an aristocratic mansion with many rooms and a peaceful garden on the outskirts of La Châtre village, which inspired the scenario often described in her novels. George Sand, born in Paris in the early 19th century, came to live at her grandmother's house as a child. From Chateauroux it's just a short trip to La Brenne, a little-known region that few tourists visit, except for the elite band of nature lovers who travel with sleeping bags and sleep under the stars. There are no trees, just scrub, moors, meadows, great silences and 400 ponds in this nook where unspoiled nature has an austere, melancholic charm. Every so often, scattered over the wide open spaces, there's a cottage, a castle, like the splendid castle of Azay-le-Ferron, or a secluded village. To the north of La Brenne are Bouges Castle and Valençay Castle, still in the gentle Berry countryside. Fields and forests lead to the discreet elegance of Bouges Castle, a severe square of pale Touraine stone with a classic beauty, devoid of pinnacles, in perfect Louis XV style. It recalls the Trianon at Versailles, partly because of the antique furnishings, collected in a lifetime's research by the last owners, M. and Mme. Viguier, who bought it in 1917.

18 bottom left The mansion of George Sand, in the Berry countryside, where the author lived as a child and later took refuge for long periods of her life.

18 right George Sand's intense look in a portrait at her Nohant mansion.

19 Meillant Castle, shrouded in the green cloak of the forest of the same name, was more defensive than romantic. A flamboyant Gothic polygonal tower can be seen on the inner side of the castle.

GRACE AND STRENGTH: AINAY-LE-VIEIL CASTLE

Ainay-le-Vieil is the southernmost castle in the Loire Valley. The thick octagonal walls of this intact medieval fortress surround the Renaissance grace of the central building, added centuries later, next to the 16th-century Renaissance tower. It is still inhabited by the descendants of Charles de Chevenon de Bigny, the noble knight who bought the property from the Lord of Culan in 1467. It houses historical relics associated with Colbert, Marie Antoinette and, still longer ago, Louis XII and Anne of Brittany. The parapets pass from tower to tower, surrounding the castle with a continuous circle of walls that has won the impressive building the nickname of "Petit Carcassonne." In the great hall is a huge fireplace, meticulously carved with symbols and the royal initials L and A against a blue background of gilded fleurs-de-lys. When spring comes, a thousand varieties of old roses bloom in the castle garden, while in summer the historic castle presents thematic exhibitions and some very popular events.

20-21 Ainay-le-Vieil, the southernmost castle in the Loire Valley, on the borders of Berry, is an extraordinary medieval fortress dating from the 14th century. Massive towers intersect the polygonal design of the outer walls, which enclose the attractive inner courtyard of the castle, with its Renaissance tower and beautifully furnished interior. The castle has belonged for five centuries to the descendants of Charles de Chevenon de Bigny, the noble knight who bought the property from the Lord of Culan in 1467.

THE RESIDENCE OF BEAUTIFUL DUCHESS: VALENÇAY CASTLE

22 top and 22-23 Standing at the end of an avenue of plane trees, beyond a monumental gateway, Valençay Castle features classical lines intersected by the great central Renaissance- style keep. Much altered over the centuries, it was transformed by Talleyrand de Périgord into a magnificent gentleman's residence.

A few miles away, Valençay Castle bears witness to the splendors of the First Empire. "Lord of Talleyrand, it is my wish that you purchase a beautiful residence where you can receive the diplomatic corps and foreigners accredited to Paris," said Napoleon to his prime minister in 1803. Talleyrand did not need to be asked twice. At Valençay he found a ruined 16th-century castle, built by Jacques d'Estampes, with an east wing added in the 17th century. He transformed it into that perfection of style and furnishing that can still be admired today by moving from room to room along the grandiose first-floor gallery and looking out over the park, where deer graze. Napoleon paid most of the price so that he could use Valençay Castle himself. In fact, he used it for six years to accommodate the Spanish king Ferdinand VII, who lost his throne through the emperor's fault. On regaining possession of the castle in 1814, Talleyrand refurbished the interior, and after the Congress of Vienna went to live there permanently with his niece by marriage, Dorothée, duchess of Dino. The grandiose palace, which has remained intact since the early 19th century, witnessed 20 years of balls, receptions, literary salons and meetings of the leading contemporary figures in politics and art.

22 bottom The halls of Valençay Castle contain antique furniture and original paintings, like the splendid oval frame containing the portrait of Princess Bénévent of Vigée-Lebrun.

23 top The magnificent collection of paintings at Valençay includes a portrait of the famous minister Talleyrand (left), and one of Victoire Alexandrine Eléonore de Damas, countess of Talleyrand-Périgord, who lived in the late 18th century (center) and was the mother of Charles Maurice Talleyrand, portrayed by Prud'hon (right).

24-25 Talleyrand de Périgord had to give up his lovely residence at Valençay between 1808 and 1814 to Ferdinand VII, King of Spain, who was exiled there after being deposed by Napoleon. Visitors can see his chamber (large photo), in First Empire style, then proceed along the large gallery on the first floor to other magnificently furnished rooms like the Blue Room (bottom left) and the cabinet de toilette (top right).

26 and 27 Napoleon's prime minister, Talleyrand de Périgord, regained possession of his castle in 1814 and partly renovated the interior decoration. Some of the most interesting rooms are the ground-floor hall containing the table around which the signatories of the Congress of Vienna sat (left-hand page), the Great Hall (top left), the Portrait Gallery (top right), and the Prince's Chamber (bottom).

28-29 The Renaissance tower by Michelangelo's pupil, Fra Giocondo, and a window in flamboyant Gothic style stand out on the south façade of Meillant Castle. The defensive structure of the castle, which is still inhabited, can be clearly seen from the entrance moat. The building contains a wealth of furnishings, halls and chambers with painted coffered ceilings.

FRA GIOCONDO'S LOVELY TOWER: MEILLANT CASTLE

Meillant Castle, enveloped in the green mantle of the forest and the scent of lime trees in spring, reveals its pretty Gothic style with a lawn of strutting peacocks, glistening ponds and the "Lion" tower—a Renaissance construction by Michelangelo's pupil Fra Giocondo—that stands at the center of the façade. Remember this tower when viewing the more famous one at Blois Castle; the Italian Renaissance touch left the first trace of its brilliant harmony here. In fact, it was Charles II d'Amboise, lord of Chaumont and governor of Milan, who introduced into Meillant Castle discreet but perceptible signs of the art he had seen flourishing across the Alps. In the inner rooms, 17th-century Dutch furniture; a great banqueting hall with minstrel's gallery and tapestries made to a design by Raphael; and a spectacular dining room with a Renaissance fireplace, a gilded coffered ceiling (partly painted in bright colors) and Cordova leather wall hangings all bring to life the age of the duke of Charost, owner of the castle during the Revolution, who had a philanthropic bent. The epitaph on his tomb in the castle chapel states, "Everywhere and at all times he did nought but good."

30 top The impressive statue of Jacques-Coeur (left) stands in the heart of Bourges opposite the famous merchant adventurer's mansion (right); the Jacques-Coeur route, which takes in the major castles of the southern Loire region, is named after him.

30-31 In the austere rooms of La Chapelle d'Angillon Castle, author Alain-Fournier found his inspiration for the characters of his famous novels, including Le Grand Meaulnes.

THE LAND OF JACQUES-COEUR

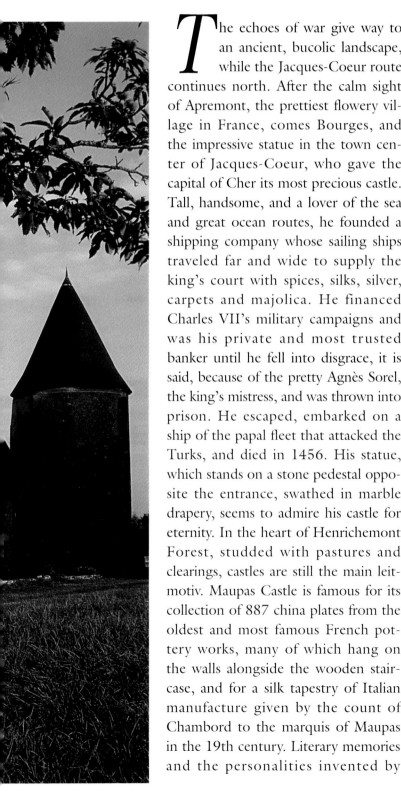

The echoes of war give way to an ancient, bucolic landscape, while the Jacques-Coeur route continues north. After the calm sight of Apremont, the prettiest flowery village in France, comes Bourges, and the impressive statue in the town center of Jacques-Coeur, who gave the capital of Cher its most precious castle. Tall, handsome, and a lover of the sea and great ocean routes, he founded a shipping company whose sailing ships traveled far and wide to supply the king's court with spices, silks, silver, carpets and majolica. He financed Charles VII's military campaigns and was his private and most trusted banker until he fell into disgrace, it is said, because of the pretty Agnès Sorel, the king's mistress, and was thrown into prison. He escaped, embarked on a ship of the papal fleet that attacked the Turks, and died in 1456. His statue, which stands on a stone pedestal opposite the entrance, swathed in marble drapery, seems to admire his castle for eternity. In the heart of Henrichemont Forest, studded with pastures and clearings, castles are still the main leitmotiv. Maupas Castle is famous for its collection of 887 china plates from the oldest and most famous French pottery works, many of which hang on the walls alongside the wooden staircase, and for a silk tapestry of Italian manufacture given by the count of Chambord to the marquis of Maupas in the 19th century. Literary memories and the personalities invented by

Alain-Fournier give a special appeal to the castle of La Chapelle D'Angillon. "I have returned to my land, the land that can only be seen by moving branches aside. I have never seen it so fresh, so concealed," wrote Alain-Fournier, when he was already beginning to imagine the adventures of *Le Grand Meaulnes* (published in English as *The Lost Domain*).

Cher, the department that, together with Indre, partly includes the ancient Berry, was a source of inspiration and peace for the author. He learned to read and write at the Epineuil-le-Fleuriel village school, enjoyed staying with his uncle in Nançay, a village comprising a few houses built around a single square, and daydreamed as a child in the great castle of La Chapelle D'Angillon. The dramatic destiny of the Princess of Clèves and the adventures of Le Grand Meaulnes, a young man lost in the memory of a mysterious kingdom where the enchanting Yvonne de Galais lived, accompany the visitor through the austere rooms of this castle. Alain-Fournier, the author of some famous novels, was born in 1886 in the village not far from the castle, but it was the great halls of the historic building that set light to his imagination. Two of them house relics of the writer's fantasy world, while others feature impressive fireplaces, beautiful paintings; a Luca della Robbia sculpture stands in the chapel, and a curious gallery is designed for *jeu de paume*, a fashionable game that was the forerunner of tennis.

SMALL WORLDS,
SPECIAL ATMOSPHERES

32-33 The gentle Berry countryside and the thick Ivoy Forest surround La Verrerie Castle, with its Renaissance portico in the inner courtyard, and rooms furnished with antique furniture and damask fabrics. Some of the rooms are reserved for paying guests who would like to spend a night in the magical atmosphere of a great château.

The land veined by the Cher River still encloses small worlds and an atmosphere of stillness: sleepy villages, roads that disappear into the countryside, abbeys, castles and landscapes untouched by the passage of time. The gentle countryside of Berry leads to the castle of La Verrerie. The Scots were at home here, because Charles VII gave this solitary castle to James Stuart in 1422. They kept it until 1683, when Louis XIV donated it to Countess Louise de Keroualle, Duchess of Portsmouth, and Charles II's mistress. In 1843 a descendent gave it to an ancestor of the present owners, the De Vogüé family. Nested in the greenery of Ivoy Forest is the classic castle with turrets, Renaissance porticoes, richly decorated halls, secret archives, huge, silent grounds, and a stream to provide silvery highlights. Visitors can admire the Gothic chapel, the reception rooms, the billiard room and the library. Some rooms are set aside for paying guests who wish to spend a night as a king amid velvets and canopies, ancestral portraits, tapestries and antique furniture. The world of fishing also appears on a royal frame. A few miles from Gien stands the lonely gray castle of La Buissière, already a fortress in the 12th century. Since 1962 the castle has housed the Fishing Museum, which contains exhibits of all kinds: fossil fish, silver fish, stuffed fish, sculpted fish, drawings of fish.

ANNE DE BEAUJEU'S RESIDENCE: GIEN CASTLE

The history of this small town, which stretches along the banks of the Loire, is closely linked to that of its castle, the first of those overlooking the Loire if the route of the famous river is followed towards the sea. The castle, standing high above the river at a point where the view is limitless, has offered hospitality to Joan of Arc among others. Before attending the coronation of Charles VII, the famous heroine spent a night praying in the wing of the castle now named after her, the only surviving part of the original feudal building.

The castle, overlooking Gien and the Loire, was built of brick and stone for Louis XI's daughter Anne de Beaujeu, Countess of Gien, in 1484. Francis I, Henri II, Charles IX and Henri III all stayed here. It survived unscathed the bombing of the Second World War, which razed the red-roofed town to the ground.

Since 1952 the castle has housed the Hunting Museum, which contains 15 rooms full of weapons of all ages, costumes, rare collections of buttons inspired by the hunt, works of art associated with the subject, tapestries, majolica, watercolors, lithographs, paintings by François Desportes, the famous animal painter to Louis XIV and Louis XV, and the Claude Hettier de Boislambert Collection of 500 hunting trophies. As well as the castle and its museum, Gien also offers another interesting attraction: the ceramic works founded in 1821 by Englishman Thomas Hulm, known as Hall, who wished to introduce the manufacture of fine English china into France. He found the right kind of clay for the purpose near Gien, while wood from the great forest of Orléans stoked the kilns that produced Gien blue, a color that remains inimitable today.

34 top Gien Castle, the first of the castles overlooking the Loire as the course of the famous river is followed, was built on the foundations of a hunting lodge erected for Charlemagne. Its involvement with hunting thus has ancient origins, and still continues today. The castle houses the magnificent Hunting Museum, which includes some lovely tapestries like the one woven following a cartoon by Laurent Guyot (right).

34-35 The large hall featuring paintings by François Desportes (1661–1743), with its mighty woodwork, contains numerous works by this famous animal painter who worked at the court of Louis XIV and Louis XV.

SULLY,
A ROMANTIC CASTLE

Sully Castle, a good example of defensive architecture on the border between Berry and Sologne, rises from the water like a romantic vision on the left bank of the Loire and its tributary, the Sange. The great hunting parties of yesteryear took place here, in the huge wooded Sologne Forest. The square tower at the entrance, the round tower on the southeastern side and the keep date back to the 15th century. From the knoll visitors can admire the castle, the park and the moats. Amid the greenery stands the marble statue of the duke of Sully, with a laurel wreath and the marshal of France baton. The Guard Room, with its coffered Vosges wood ceilings, leads to the Great Hall where Voltaire, exiled here after libeling the Prince Regent, Philippe d'Orléans, staged some of his plays between 1716 and 1719. Near the Great Hall, separated by a solid iron door, is the oratory, followed by the King's Chamber, with tapestries, a four-poster bed with blue canopy and wood-paneled walls. Finally, 40 steps lead up to the top floor, where visitors can see the framework of the roof: a brilliantly engineered wooden skeleton. This very tall pitched roof, which dates from the late 14th century, has undergone catapult attacks, but has always withstood them and is still there, like a great upside-down ship's hull, waiting to be admired for its latticework of beams and the unusual design of its roof.

36-37 The romantic sight of Sully Castle, a good example of defensive architecture, rises from the water on the border between Berry and Sologne. Among its attractions are the Guard Room, with its ceiling painted in pure gold, the King's Chamber—with tapestries portraying scenes from classical mythology and a blue damask canopy to match the walls—and the extraordinary roof frame, with its upturned-hull shape.

A WORLD PRESERVED IN STONE

Tourists who travel through the Loire Valley or merely hear stories about its magnificent residences wonder why so many castles and princely residences were built there. Why by the Loire, and not the Seine, for example, or other no less famous rivers? Because the Loire Valley, with its warm, dry climate, has always been the garden of France; because along the riverbanks there were already fortresses and castles able to accommodate royal guests; and because in the 15th century the king's political survival depended on the resistance offered along the Loire border by the dukes of Berry and Orléans in the south against the English and in the north against the Burgundians. Even after his accession to the throne, Charles VII remained fascinated by the climate and landscape of the gentle Loire Valley. After the Treaty of Troyes (1420), which stripped him of his kingdom, he lived at Chinon, Loches and Amboise with the sole title of Roi de Bourges. Following the legendary liberation by Joan of Arc of Orléans, besieged by the English, in May 1429, Charles VII began to win back his kingdom, but when he was finally able to return to liberated Paris on November 12, 1437, he only stayed a few days. Homesick, he took the court back to Chinon, preferring to pass his life in the gentle Touraine, where he had been bewitched by the beautiful Agnès Sorel. His son, Louis XI, who grew up at Loches Castle, though a restless wanderer by nature, nearly always lived in the castles of Amboise and Plessis-lez-Tours. Charles VIII, who was fond of Amboise, also had no desire to transfer the court to Paris.

After his marriage he spent a year at Langeais Castle; then, on his return from the Italian campaign in 1495, he decided to live at Amboise and convert the castle into a modern residence, for which purpose he summoned skilled craftsmen and artists from Italy. His successor, Louis XII, also chose the Loire, as did Francis I who lived at Blois Castle in the early years of his reign. Three years after his coronation began the construction of his own castle, Chambord. Today, in the summer, many castles stage historical reenactments; sound-and-light shows, pageants and plays to familiarize the public with the history of the best-known castles. The Francis I route follows the ancient road traveled by the king on his way to Italy, while the Vallée des Rois route leads to royal residences and sleepy old-world villages. Even without following a set route, the castles follow one after another. The castle of Chenonceau, the best known and most visited, recounts tales of love and the revenge of betrayed mistresses, while Villandry's charm focuses on its gardens. Cheverny is still inhabited, and the pack of dogs used for fox hunting in the autumn can be seen in its avenues in the afternoons.

Then there's Azay-le-Rideau; Langeais with its tapestries; Ussé, so unreal that it inspired the fairy tale of Sleeping Beauty; Blois, where French history was made and the duke of Guise was assassinated; Chinon, which featured in the destiny of Joan of Arc; Amboise, linked with Italy because of its association with Leonardo da Vinci; and Chambord, which, with its huge size, its 380 chimneys and 406 rooms, exemplifies and concludes the saga of the Loire castles.

38 top left Feudal towers and outer walls give Chaumont Castle, which stands on a hill overlooking the Loire, the appearance of an impregnable fortress. The castle has an air of mystery, the legacy of its association, at the height of its splendor, with a court astronomer who was more of a magician and fortune-teller than a scientist.

38 top right Villandry Castle is a magnificent residence, but its fame is not so much due to the interior as to its magnificent flower and vegetable gardens, whose colors change with the seasons and the crops. These gardens were inspired by ancient documents written by medieval monks.

38-39 Little Azay-le-Rideau Castle, framed by a romantic natural setting of rare beauty, overlooks the Indre River amid lush vegetation with plane trees, lime trees and tall oaks.

40 top *The Salle des Gardes at Langeais Castle, with its classical layout and furnishings: great brass chandeliers, a pale stone fireplace, paneled walls and exposed beams on the ceiling.*

THE INFLUENCE
OF ITALIAN ART

The Loire Valley is an immense setting that, in a way, belongs to the marvelous period of the Italian Renaissance. In the stone friezes, spiral staircases, windows lighting the halls, and castle porticoes – almost everywhere, in fact – Italian influence has left the unmistakable imprint of its grandeur. The façade of Valençay Castle has the same scenic perfection as the 15th century palazzi of Florence, the staircase of Blois Castle repeats the floral motifs of many Tuscan portals, and the names of many famous personalities are linked with the Loire Valley. One such personality was Catherine de Médicis who, when she married Henri II, brought to France the art of good living, the gaiety of the *volta* (a rather daring dance that delighted the court), and the elegance and taste of the great balls and banquets held in Florence under the Médicis.

Another was Leonardo da Vinci, who ended his days at the castle of Clos-Lucé in Amboise, given to him by Francis I. He arrived from Florence, his mules loaded with the canvases of the Mona Lisa, St. Anne and John the Baptist. He warmed himself by the fire in the Great Hall, and in the peace of that retreat organized magnificent parties for his French king, creating flying machines and robots that, when struck on the chest, released pure white lilies and perfumed roses onto the guests.

After his death and the return of Francis I from the Battle of Pavia (1528), the time was ripe for the king to return to the capital. The destiny of the Loire as the headquarters of the court was over. Chambord Castle was finished, and from then on was only used for holidays and hunting parties. However, distant sounds still seem to issue from that kingdom of keeps, pinnacles and parapets: the rustle of silk, the clank of armor, dance steps and the gentle notes of lutes and rebecs.

40-41 Chambord: a sight that seems like a mirage. Standing alone at the end of a huge park, Chambord Castle incarnates the megalomaniac dream of a king who wished to conclude the age of the splendors and legends of the Loire Valley with the most magnificent castle ever built on the riverbanks.

41 right Blois Castle stands in the heart of the town of the same name on the right bank of the Loire, about 37 miles from Orléans. In the 15th century it was the favorite royal residence of Louis XII, who ordered large-scale extension work.

IN THE FOOTSTEPS OF JOAN OF ARC: CHINON CASTLE

Orléans commemorates Joan of Arc every May 8, when 1,000 banners fly from Fort des Tourelles to Place St. Croix. The famous Maid of Orléans, played by a young girl, walks at the head of a great procession. This pageant commemorates the day in 1429 when Joan arrived to liberate the city from the English siege. Her "crusade" had set out from Chinon Castle, where Charles VII had taken refuge after escaping from Paris. Joan arrived there on March 9, 1429, escorted by six men, asking to be brought before the king. It was a dramatic time for France. Henry IV was king of England and king of Paris; Charles VII was only king of Bourges. The states general of the central and southern provinces, which had remained loyal to him, had decided to finance the war against the English, but the dauphin hesitated. Joan waited for two days, praying, until she was eventually received in the Throne Room (sadly now partly demolished; only the monumental fireplace remains, together with what, according to legend, is the footprint of the famous heroine). King Charles VII, who had exchanged clothes with a courtier, was concealed among 300 costumed nobles. But Joan was not to be deceived. She walked straight up to the king, embraced his knees and said, "My name is Joan, and I am sent by the king of Heaven to tell you that you will be crowned true king of the French at Rheims Cathedral." The king doubted her word and sent the girl to Poitiers for medical examinations, to establish whether she was a witch or an envoy of God. Eleven days later, convinced by the results, Charles VII permitted Joan of Arc to march at the head of his army against the English. Until 1450 Chinon Castle on the Vienne, a tributary of the Loire, was the headquarters of the court, which later moved to Amboise and Blois. The castle was used once more by Louis XII in 1498 to receive Cesare Borgia, sent by the Pope to deliver the papal bull annulling his marriage with Joan of France so that he could wed Anne of Brittany, thus uniting Brittany and France. The chronicles tell of a grandiose entrance of 68 mules bearing trunks, crates and chairs covered with gold brocade, accompanied by pages, minstrels and drummer-boys. Men and animals draped in brocades and crimson velvets preceded Duke Cesare, who rode a horse decked out with precious stones and pearls. The duke's costume was so precious and studded with gems and diamonds that it "shone like a lighthouse." The duke, son of the Pope, was received with full honors, although it was already known that as cardinal he had been his sister's lover and his brother's murderer. Little now remains of Chinon Castle apart from the grandiose foundations and some towers, including the Tour de l'Horloge with the bell, Marie Javelle, which has struck the hours since 1399, and the Tour d'Argenton, built towards the end of the 15th century, in the location where Louis XI is said to have held his prisoners.

The king's mistress, Agnès Sorel, lived in the adjacent Coudray Castle, which the sovereign reached via secret underground passages. Joan of Arc was held prisoner in the tower of the same building, as were the Templars, whose heartrending messages can still be read on the walls, centuries later. The countryside around Tours is characterized by precious vineyards that produce the red Chinon, Bourgeuil and Saint Nicolas and the white MontLouis and Vouvray wines that accompany the gastronomic delights of the Loire Valley.

42-43 Seen from the Vienne River, Chinon Castle reveals the defensive and military features of what was one of the most famous fortresses of the 15th century. Here the dauphin of France took refuge when he left Paris during a night of terror; Joan of Arc came to the castle too, to implore the king to grant her the honor of marching at the head of his troops against the English army besieging Orléans.

43 top Chinon, with its slate roofs and the web of narrow lanes at the foot of the castle, offers some major tourist attractions, such as a famous wine and a costume fair that, every August, takes the small town four centuries back in time.

43 right Built on a crag where the Romans had already established a castrum (camp) because of its strategic position on the river, Chinon Castle still has some towers that demonstrate that a veritable citadel, not just a castle, once stood at the summit of the village.

43 bottom Partly destroyed over the centuries, Chinon Castle is more famous for its magnificent architectural design than for its wealth of interior decorations, which include some magnificent Aubusson tapestries.

44-45 and 44 top
Ussé Castle still
breathes the enchanted
atmosphere of Sleeping
Beauty, *the fairy tale
by Charles Perrault
that made it famous.
Its towers, with their
gray conical roofs, and
the thick forest all
around have helped
preserve the magic of
this spot over the
centuries.*

45 bottom *The
world-famous Ussé
Castle is now a
favorite destination
of couples looking for
a romantic setting
for their wedding.*

USSÉ: SLEEPING BEAUTY'S CASTLE

*U*ssé Castle, an enchanting mixture of pinnacles and pointed turrets, is known as Sleeping Beauty's castle. It was an ancient fortress when it belonged to Jean de Bueil, who married a daughter of Charles VII and Agnès Sorel. Work later began on converting it into a less severe home, bristling with towers and pinnacles. It was such an enchanted castle that it inspired Charles Perrault to write his famous fairy tale; so magical that it has caught the imagination of the Japanese, who travel halfway across the world to get married in this romantic setting. The castle is quadrangular in shape, bounded at the corners by keeps and pinnacles. However, like nearly all those in the Loire Valley, the appearance of the building and the original architectural plans, which date back to the 15th and early 16th centuries, were changed by the various owners. The interior of Ussé Castle is richly decorated, and its rooms, with their 18th-century tapestries and 17th- and 18th-century furniture, constitute veritable museums. Some tapestries also hang on the walls of the long gallery, with its black-and-white tiled floor. Paintings of famous schools line the main staircase and the Salle Royale. A rare piece of Renaissance furniture inlaid with ivory occupies almost an entire wall of the *cabinet florentin*. The chapel, which has a nave with no aisles, was built between 1523 and 1535. It contains 16th-century wooden choir-stalls and an enameled majolica Virgin attributed to Luca della Robbia.

45 top Two ancient cedars (legend has it that they were planted by Chateaubriand) protect the 16th-century chapel. The interior, which has a nave but no aisles, is decorated with wooden choir-stalls dating from the period when the chapel was built. However, the most valuable item is an enameled terra-cotta Madonna made by Luca della Robbia around the mid-15th century.

46-47 *The wealth of the interior of Ussé Castle matches the charm of the exterior. The furnishings, especially the tapestries and furniture, enhance the magnificence of the 18th-century galleries and halls. The Aubusson tapestries and those by Flemish craftsmen depicting rural scenes are particularly exquisite. Ancient weapons and paintings of a good artistic level alternate with Italian furniture, like the rare ivory-inlaid specimen in* the cabinet florentin.

MORE TALES
OF LOVE AND WAR:
LOCHES CASTLE

48 top Some major historical events took place here, like the meeting at the castle entrance, depicted by Alexandre Millin du Perreux, between Joan of Arc and Charles VII, when the famous maid returned victorious from the siege of Orléans in 1429.

48 bottom Charles VII gave Loches Castle to his mistress, Agnès Sorel, who is depicted in a famous painting by Jean Fouquet that shows a naked breast escaping provocatively from the laces of a corset.

Between one military campaign and the next, the sovereigns who lived by the Lòire devoted a great deal of time to feasting, jousting and love affairs. They had mistresses whose names have gone down in history and who, in exchange for their loyalty, were rewarded with castles and riches. Charles VII and Agnès Sorel were bound by a true passion, and a castle was the reward for every child she bore (four in all). Loches Castle, the largest, had existed since the 6th century with the name of Castellum. In 840 Charles the Bald gave it to a loyal knight, who passed it on to a niece who married Foulques the Black of the House of Anjou. The castle has an exceptional defensive system of walls and towers. It underwent lengthy sieges in the 13th century in the battle fought for possession of Touraine between the Plantagenet King Henry II of England and his sons Richard the Lionheart and John Lackland against Philip Augustus. In the 15th century it became the favorite residence of Charles VII and Agnès Sorel. She died in 1450, and her body lies in an alabaster sarcophagus in the tower that bears her name. A portrait of the king's mistress in another room (a copy of the original, which is in a private collection) shows the delicate grace of her body and a naked breast escaping provocatively from the laces of a corset. From Loches it is just a short walk to Montrésor, one of the prettiest villages in France. The most famous lord of the manor was Imbert de Bastarnay, who bought the existing fortress in 1493 and converted it into the pretty castle that now belongs to the descendants of Count Branicki, the Polish nobleman who bought the property in the 19th century. A friend of Napoleon III, he was a leading financier and a collector of valuable works of art, now on display: paintings by Raphael, Caravaggio and Veronese, silverware belonging to the ancient kings of Poland, hunting trophies, jewelry and furniture from the Italian Renaissance period.

AGNES SOREL

48-49 and 49 top The warm light of sunset mellows the austere design of Loches Castle. More of a defensive bulwark than a romantic castle, it has survived intact over the centuries, with its famous tower,

the royal gate, and the chancellery built by the Counts of Anjou. The Counts, who were among the first owners of the castle, also ruled over the town, with its narrow medieval lanes huddled at the foot of the crag.

50 top left Huge fireplaces, shining armor and splendid windows give the interior of the castle a unique, fascinating atmosphere.

50 bottom right It was in this room that Joan of Arc delivered her famous speech to King Charles VII in June 1429, urging him to go to Rheims to be crowned king of the French.

50-51 The beautiful Agnès Sorel had a long love affair with Charles VII. Her tomb, watched over by an angel, lies in a tower of the castle.

51 bottom Pages of history have been written at Loches Castle, from the long love affair between Charles VII and the lovely Agnès Sorel to the imprisonment of Cardinal La Balue, counselor to Louis XI, who betrayed the king

to Charles the Bold. He was imprisoned in the Martelet, the gloomy prison with three tiers of cells (cachots) constructed in the Tour Neuve, where Ludovico il Moro, duke of Milan, was also held prisoner by Louis XII.

52-53 and 52 top
Saumur Castle, a
quadrangle bounded
by polygonal towers
with conical slate
roofs, stands on a
rocky promontory
that seems to watch
over the last stretch of
the Loire as it flows
towards the sea.

THE CASTLES OF ANJOU

Here the Loire enters Anjou, and before reaching the sea passes by two more famous castles, those of Saumur and Angers. The castle of Saumur, the town that contains the leading French riding school, stands on a rocky promontory. The castle, a quadrilateral with polygonal corner towers, conical roofs of bluish slate and Renaissance-Gothic decorations on a visibly medieval structure, is reached by walking up narrow, steep streets, until the effort is rewarded by a superb view and a visit to the richly decorated rooms. The castle dates from the late 14th century, although its appearance reveals some later additions.

It was the Italian Bartolomeo who built the outer fortifications, which herald the form of the typical Vauban ramparts. A Huguenot stronghold in the 17th century, then a barracks and a penitentiary, it was restructured at the turn of this century and houses three museums: the Decorative Arts Museum, Toy Soldier Museum and Equestrian Museum, which displays harnesses, trappings and uniforms. Although it has the resources and dynamism of a big city, Angers, with its close-knit network of squares and pedestrian precincts and its clusters of houses over 500 years old, looks like a large village. At the center is its symbol: the squat pentagonal fortress erected by Blanche of Castille, mother of St. Louis, in the early 13th century as a bulwark against the restless Breton populations. Later, at the end of the 13th century, residential buildings, hanging gardens and a chapel for the ducal family of Anjou were added. What was once the residence of the poet-prince René contains the famous *Apocalypse*, about 118 yards of allegorical scenes made with the tapestry technique by 14th-century artists. It has six sections, each divided into 14 episodes, featuring red-blue shades, dragons with huge heads, quadrupeds ridden by Death, sea creatures with macabre features and crude representations of the human face. This is the best visiting card for the itinerary that starts from the castle and continues as far as the *"promenade du bout du monde,"* leading the visitor to the attractive historic buildings in the town center.

53 left and top right Saumur Castle dates from the late 14th century, but like all those in the famous valley it was altered over the centuries and also served various purposes: it was a Huguenot stronghold in the 17th century, then a barracks, and then a penitentiary. It now houses three museums: the Decorative Arts Museum, the Toy Soldier Museum and the Equestrian Museum.

53 bottom right The mighty Angers Castle, a squat pentagonal fortress, was built by Blanche of Castille, mother of Saint Louis, in the early 13th century, to protect the area, which was threatened by the restless Breton populations.

A LADY'S ROMANTIC DREAM: AZAY-LE-RIDEAU

54-55 *The greenery of the park contrasts with the silvery veil of the Indre River as it flows past Azay-le-Rideau Castle, creating a romantic atmosphere. An enchanting blend of pinnacles and sharp turrets, the castle houses valuable works of art such as a 16th-century portrait by an unknown artist of a young woman reading, a portrait of Louis XIV standing, and a 16th-century portrait of the duke of Guise, nicknamed le Balafré (Scarface).*

*I*n the spot where the road from Tours to Chinon crosses the Indre, a left-hand tributary of the Loire, once stood the watchtower of Azay-le-Rideau. This was a medieval fortification surrounded by a deep moat and manned by a garrison of Burgundian soldiers. For 100 years it was no more than a pile of rubble, after Charles VII set fire to the entire village and the fortified tower in 1418, also killing the soldiers of the garrison, to take revenge for the insults he had received. In 1518 the court financier, Gilles Berthelot, treasurer to Francis I, bought the property and commissioned architect Étienne Rousseau to erect a castle in Renaissance style in a pretty spot where the Indre formed a small lake. The work lasted 10 years, until 1529, and was directed by the financier's wife, Philippa Lesbahy. The result was a residence designed for the pure pleasure of living in it, with no defensive purposes. It was built partly on the water, its romantic white image reflected in the lake, with conical towers, slate roofs and pretty ornaments outside and the great right-angled staircase inside. It was Philippa Lesbahy who gave the residence the elegant furnishings it still retains: drawing rooms full of paintings, a collection of blue majolica plates, and walls hung with Gobelin tapestries. That is why the castle is one of the most beautiful in the Loire Valley and was liked so much by Francis I who, taking advantage of a

conspiracy, had no hesitation in confiscating it and exiling the owner, Berthelot. In the King's Chamber, where Francis I almost certainly stayed, is a great fireplace with the initials F and C (standing for queen Claude). It is followed by the Green Room, named after the huge green damask four-poster bed dating from the 17th century, the Red Room, where crimson damask still prevails in the furnishings, and the Banqueting Hall, with its huge fireplace and valuable Brussels tapestries.

56-57 Great tapestries hang from the walls of the magnificent Renaissance-style rooms of Azay-le-Rideau Castle, featuring great fireplaces, light, vaulted kitchens and a simple but elegant main staircase leading to the upper floors. It was Mme Philippa Lesbahy in the 16th century who gave the castle the gentle, cozy air it still retains today. Designed as a medieval fortification, it was reduced to a pile of ruins in 1418, and finally converted to a nobleman's residence in 1529.

58 More beautiful rooms in Azay-le-Rideau castle bear witness to the famous personalities who stayed there: the Salle à Manger, decorated in Henri II style (top right), the chamber of Francis I with the royal emblem of the salamander engraved on the fireplace (left), and the Blue Room (bottom right), which belonged to Maréchal de la Barre, who was killed in the siege of Nice in 1705.

59 A plain four-poster bed, an original marble table, wall hangings and golden yellow curtains with the most popular flower patterns, and a monumental fireplace are the few concessions to luxury in the simple, cozy bedroom of Francis I.

A CASTLE OF WEAPONRY AND LOVE: LANGEAIS

60 The marriage of Charles VIII to Anne of Brittany was celebrated in Langeais Castle in 1491. The hall where the wedding took place, with its great tapestries and beamed ceiling, remains intact (bottom right). The royal bedchamber, with its four-poster bed (bottom left), exemplifies the furnishings typical of great 15th-century mansions. In Langeais Castle, 13 chambers are hung with 15th- and 16th-century Flemish tapestries. The chapel (top left) has the typical inverted-hull-shaped ceiling.

*I*n the numerous castles that follow the Loire Valley from Gien to Saumur, the desire for beauty replaced the need for defensive security in the century of the Renaissance. Langeais Castle, situated to the west of Tours by the riverside, is the only medieval fortress that has remained intact and has never been changed over the centuries by rebuilding work. After passing through the main door visitors enter the inner courtyard, where they see the ruins of a high wall, part of the ancient fortress built in 994 by Foulques the Red, founder of the Anjou Dynasty, a farsighted politician and strategist, but also a treacherous, cynical feudal brigand.

Langeais Castle and the entire province of Touraine passed to the Counts of Anjou in the 11th century, then to the Plantagenets. During the Hundred Years' War it was occupied by the English on various occasions. The present castle was built by Louis XI. Charles VIII and Anne of Brittany were married there in 1491. The chronicles tell of the magnificent procession that escorted the future bride, clad in a gold and velvet robe decorated with 160 sables, into the king's presence, and of the magnificent banquet with flocks of doves, meat pies, patties containing warblers, quails and turtle doves, and boiled capons covered with fine gold. After the wedding the severe feudal castle must have seemed gloomy to the 15-year-old

bride, who only a year later preferred to move with the court to Amboise Castle. Since then, Langeais Castle has never reappeared in the history books, but the austere style of its walls, the rooms hung with 16th-century tapestries and the valuable antique furniture beautifully recreate the atmosphere of its legendary past.

61 Proud and solemn in its feudal armor, Langeais Castle has survived the ravages of time and war unharmed. The castle, whose features are typical of late 15th-century defensive architecture, overlooks the Loire and the roofs of the village below.

GREAT HISTORICAL EVENTS: AMBOISE

62-63 *Medieval and Renaissance styles are blended in the majestic Amboise Castle, with its stone friezes, spiral staircases and windows casting light on halls and porticoes. Standing high above the Loire, the castle still seems to control its strategic position as a defensive bulwark by the ford. For centuries that was its function, with the result that its walls have witnessed a great deal of history.*

Amboise Castle is one of the most important castles in the Loire Valley because of the historical events that took place there and the role it played in introducing Italian art into France. Its origins date from the Gallo-Roman period. In 500 Clovis, king of the Franks, met Alaric, king of the Visigoths, there. They challenged one another to a chivalrous duel, and Alaric was killed. Later, the importance of Amboise grew with the construction of the bridge over the Loire, because there were only seven bridges between Gien and Angers, and anyone who controlled them, thus enabling troops to cross

the river, would control the entire region.

The promontory of Chatelliers, a spur of rock at the end of which stands Amboise Castle, was always a crossroads because of its ideal position at the confluence of the Loire and the Amasse. The bridge, town and castle were owned by the Counts of Amboise until the mid-15th century, when Charles VII ordered them to be confiscated in favor of his son Louis XI, who took up residence there with his wife, Charlotte of Savoy. Thus Charles VIII, who became king at the age of 13 and was already a courageous commander by the age of 20, was born at Amboise. On his return from the Italian campaign in 1494 he brought with him not only furniture, carpets and fabrics but also Italian artists, painters, tailors and craftsmen who soon changed the face of the castle. Amboise was transformed.

64-65 *Charles VIII, who became king at the age of 13 and was already an able commander at 20, was born at Amboise. He left Amboise to fight in Italy, and on returning to the banks of the Loire in 1494, decided to renovate his castle in the Renaissance style he had so admired south of the Alps. The new architectural canons are evident at Amboise Castle, where flashes of Gothic style, still evident, for example, in the Round Arch Room (left), blend with the new Renaissance influences (right).*

Landscape gardener Pacello Mercogliano created the first Italianate garden; brilliant architects and sculptors embellished the residence in accordance with Renaissance style; and hundreds of Turkish carpets and tapestries from Flanders and Damascus adorned the magnificent rooms.

A solemn tournament was held to celebrate its renovation. On April 7, 1498, Easter Eve, Charles VIII, accompanied by his wife, Anne of Brittany, went to the Hacquelebac Gallery on the way to the tournament field. Charles forgot to bend his head, and though he was by no means tall, he accidentally hit his forehead against the entrance architrave. He still watched the tournament, but then fell into a coma and died at 9 o'clock the same evening. He was succeeded by his cousin Louis d'Orléans, who became King Louis XII, married Charles' widow, Anne of Brittany, and gave Amboise to Louise of Savoy, mother of Francis I of Angoulême, who was heir to the throne. When he became king in 1515, Francis I demonstrated a particular fondness for the castle where he had spent his childhood. He completed the wing begun by Louis XII and summoned Leonardo da Vinci from Italy.

66-67 *Magnificent furnishings and original paintings decorate the rooms of Amboise Castle, like the room in Louis Philippe style dominated by crimson fabrics and upholstery.*

67 *The hall is dominated by the great portraits hanging on the walls, including those of the duke of Orléans (top left) and Maria Amelia of Bourbon (top right).*

68 top *The elegant Salle aux Poutres, designed and decorated between the 15th and 16th centuries, contains exquisite tapestries, beamed ceilings and priceless antique furniture.*

68 left and 69 top and bottom *The classic, severe style of the Renaissance period dominates these rooms of Amboise Castle; a good example is provided by the chamber of Henri II, with the large tapestries on the walls, great fireplaces, and four-poster beds.*

68-69 The classical
style of furnishing
characteristic of all
the Loire chateaux
can be seen in the
Salle des Gardes, with
its Gothic ceilings,
and the rooms
adjacent to it.

70-71 Amboise Castle not only provided the venue for some major historical events; above all, it provided the base from which Renaissance art was introduced into France because the great Leonardo da Vinci (shown here in a marble bust at top left) moved from Milan to spend the rest of his life there. His tomb is in St. Hubert's Chapel, constructed in flamboyant Gothic style with large windows and a richly decorated portal.

72-73 *After loading some precious canvases, including the Mona Lisa, onto mules, Leonardo da Vinci left Florence for Amboise at the age of 64. Here Francis I is shown awaiting the great artist, to whom he donated Clos-Lucé Castle, where he spent the rest of his life.*

His spirit can be felt in every room, such as the bedroom with the four-poster bed and large stone fireplace where he died, and in the collection on the basement of scale models of brilliant machines that he designed and about which he left detailed notes.

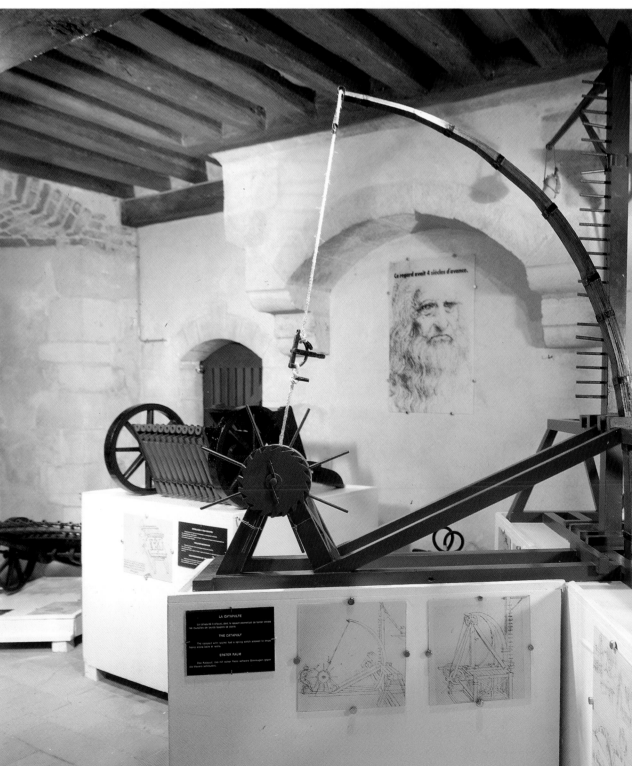

AN ARTIST'S JOURNEY
AND A KING'S FRIENDSHIP
LEONARDO DA VINCI AND FRANCIS I:
FROM AMBOISE TO CLOS-LUCÉ

Leonardo, at the age of 64, loaded the canvases of the Mona Lisa, St. Anne and John the Baptist onto mules, left Florence, and set off for Amboise with his faithful disciple, Francesco Melzi, and his servant, Battista di Villanis. Francis I received the Italian genius at Amboise, and gave him Cloux Castle (now Clos-Lucé) and an annuity of 700 gold scudos. All he required in exchange was the pleasure of conversation with him. From 1516, Leonardo spent the last years of his life in the Loire Valley, masterminding splendid parties, masked balls and artists' conferences, and continuing his studies of engineering and anatomy. He lies in St. Hubert's Chapel in Amboise Castle. On the death of Francis I in 1547, the decline of Amboise began. In the 17th century Louis XIII visited the castle to hunt in the nearby forest, but under Louis XIV the mighty walls became grim state prisons. Amboise castle regained its past glory under Louis XV, who gave it to the duke of Choiseul, and later under Napoleon, who confiscated the castle and gave it to a member of the Directory, Roger Ducos. The latter had insufficient funds to maintain the great building and demolished part of it, but despite this mutilation, the castle still presents a faithful picture of what court life must have been like 400 years ago.

There were two mighty towers, about 22 yards tall, with spiral staircases, in which a horse could be ridden right to the top; the king's apartments, the guardroom, and a wonderful view from the large terrace over the Loire and its tributary, the Amasse, complete the picture of one of the most spectacular castles in the valley. A long walk from Amboise is the magic of Clos-Lucé Castle, the residence of Leonardo da Vinci. The king and the "painter-cum-engineer" got along extraordinarily well; both of them enthusiastically cherished fantastic dreams. Leonardo was planning to build prefabricated wooden houses for the populace, to connect all the Loire castles with a series of canals, to make flying machines with wings. His designs and intuitions were ahead of their time in a century of humanists not given to flights of fancy. The time was not yet ripe for the scientific innovations that continually issued from the mind of the great genius, and everything remained on paper. At Clos-Lucé, in the very rooms that witnessed this outpouring of ideas and the long talks between the Italian artist and his royal patron, the astonished visitor can view the collection of manuscripts and the models of machines reconstructed in accordance with Leonardo's detailed instructions.

*74-75 and 74 top
Magic and mystery
inhabit Chaumont
Castle, with its pale
stone and sloping
slate roofs, situated
just a few miles from
Amboise and Blois,
which were so
powerful in the
Middle Ages.*

A QUEEN'S DARK SECRETS: CHAUMONT

The memory of Catherine de Médicis pervades the halls of Chaumont Castle. In 1560, as widow of Henri II, she bought the castle to take her revenge for her husband's adultery and force his mistress, Diane de Poitiers, to exchange it for Chenonceau Castle, which Henri had given her in 1547, when he ascended to the throne. The beautiful Diane could hardly refuse, but did not stay long at Chaumont, preferring exile at Anet Castle, where she died seven years later, far from the gossip of the Loire Valley.

The memory of the great Catherine is still very much alive at Chaumont. Her adviser on the occult arts, the sorcerer Ruggieri, is said to have stayed there, and the existence of a room connected to a tower by a steep staircase has led to rumors of a secret hideaway where the queen and her adviser retired to conduct magic rites and interrogate the stars about the future. Catherine is said to have discovered the tragic destiny awaiting her three children and the imminent advent of the Bourbons at Chaumont. The castle stands on a hill overlooking the left bank of the river. Until the 15th century it was the feudal fortress of the Counts of Blois; it was later rebuilt with round guard towers and softened by the addition of conical roofs and Renaissance influences. It passed through the hands of various owners, including the chatelain who demolished the north wing in the 18th century to obtain a better view of the Loire, and one Le Ray who, also in the 18th century, arranged for the famous Italian pottery maker Battista Nini to stay there. The latter set up his workshop in the stables, and his great kiln in an old dovecote. He made an important contribution to the history of art by reproducing numerous copies of ceramic medallions of the most famous personalities of the period, some of which are on display in the rooms of the castle leading to the chambers of Diane, Catherine and the astrologer Ruggieri.

76-77 Chaumont Castle, the feudal fortress of the Counts of Blois until the 15th century, was later rebuilt with round watchtowers and ornamented with conical roofs and Renaissance influences.

78 The air of mystery with which Chaumont Castle was rife soon became a legend; the main centers from which this fascination still radiates are the chamber of Queen Catherine de Médicis (bottom right) in her favorite green, that of the sorcerer Ruggieri (top right), and the chapel, with its pointed stained-glass windows (top left).

79 The narrow Gothic-style staircase that runs through the heart of the castle perhaps led to the mysterious laboratory of the occult arts presided over by Ruggieri, the powerful court astrologer who predicted the death of Henri III, which put an end to the reign of the Valois dynasty.

80-81 Though it boasts three main buildings, a keep and a court of honor, Villandry Castle does not tell the stories of kings and queens. Spanish magnate Carvallo came to Villandry after the Second World War with the intention of buying the ancient castle to create a special garden.

The rooms, with the original marble checkerboard floor (bottom right), can be visited, and the architectural design of the mighty building admired, but then the visitor will inevitably be drawn to the flower gardens, the avenues lined with lime trees and the unusual vegetable garden (top left).

IN BALZAC'S LOVELY COUNTRYSIDE: VILLANDRY

Nature reigns supreme in the quiet Touraine; meadows and forests play with the silvery ribbon of the river that flows, murmurs and splashes in the royal gardens and penetrates everywhere, constituting the characteristic feature of the gentle, sunny landscape of the Loire Valley. The charm of Villandry Castle revolves around its unique gardens. The history of France has never entered its walls, nor was it ever the home of a king or a courtesan. It was built about 10 miles from Tours by Jean le Breton, prime minister of Francis I, in 1536. He constructed three horseshoe-shaped buildings opening onto the Loire Valley on the foundations of a feudal fortress that was demolished, and of which only the south keep remains. Cross windows, dormer windows with carved pediments and tall, steeply sloping slate roofs form a complex of rare harmony, although the turrets and pinnacles have not survived. A simpler style, which was later to become the Henri IV style, was beginning to predominate in monumental architecture. However, the history of the castle is of little importance at Villandry. It is the square gardens, arranged by color and obsessively well tended, that invite the visitor to roam among terraces, kitchen gardens and flower beds whose colors change from season to season. The layout of the gardens was restored to its original 16th-century design by Spanish millionaire Carvallo, who became the castle's owner after the

Second World War. After discovering the original designs by Androuet du Cerceau, the architect who created the gardens, Carvallo recreated the original structure, with three terraces built on different levels, avenues shaded by lime trees, straight paths along which flowers blossom, box hedges clipped by topiarists and the curious herbariums of the medieval monks; visitors can stroll through the garden of love and the garden of music, amid mallow and chervil, beets, cabbage seedlings and pumpkins.

83 *The ornamental gardens dedicated to love are clearly seen from the panoramic terrace. The designer intended the arrangement of the hedges to reflect the symbols of various types of love: hearts and flames represented tender love, deformed hearts delirious love, swords and daggers tragic love, and fans and letters of the alphabet elusive love.*

82 Androuet du Cerceau designed the gardens of Villandry, magnificent green spaces that still retain their original appearance, with three terraces built at different levels. The layout of the gardens not only reflects the taste of the period, but also aims to recreate a philosophical symbolism in the arrangement of hedges and floral decorations. Some very rare species, often from distant regions, were cultivated here in the 16th century.

84 *Chenonceau was built for Christine Briçonnet, given to Diane de Poitiers (portrayed as Diana the Huntress by Primaticcio, bottom left) by her lover Henri II (shown in a contemporary portrait, bottom left), reclaimed by Catherine de Médicis, and passed on to Louise of Lorraine, widow of Henri III, who spent 12 years mourning there.*

THE CASTLE OF QUEENS: CHENONCEAU

Just a stone's throw from the flourishing, idyllic rural town of Montrichard stands the most frequently visited and most romantic castle in the Loire Valley: Chenonceau, known as "the castle of six ladies" because of the role played by six chatelaines in its 400-year history. This *caprice des femmes* is famous for its five-span bridge and the two-storey gallery over the Cher, as well as the 15th-century circular keep, the gardens dedicated to Catherine and Diane, the two women who shared the king's favors, and the interior, including Diane de Poitiers' room, Catherine de Médicis' green study, and the queen's chamber, decorated with Gobelin tapestries. At different times the castle was inhabited by Mme. Catherine Briconnet, who built it with her husband, Thomas Bohier, Diane de Poitiers, who was given it by her lover Henri II, Catherine de Médicis, who reclaimed it on her husband's death, and Louise of Lorraine, widow of Henri III, who mourned her husband's death there, dressed in white according to royal protocol; she is said to have murmured nothing but prayers for 12 years.

After Louise of Lorraine, Chenonceau fell into a period of decline until Mme Dupin became its owner in the 18th century, and one of the most famous literary salons of the age developed around her and Jean-Jacques Rousseau, her son's tutor. In 1864 the castle was bought by Mme Pelouze, who meticulously restored its original design and then sold it to the present owners, the Menier family.

The grace of its design, the airy beauty of the gallery built by Catherine de Médicis and the tidy grounds once provided the romantic setting for the lives of queens and courtesans, which are recreated every summer evening in a sound-and-light show .

85 *So ethereal that it seems to glide through the blue waters of the Cher like a stone galleon, so rich in history that every corner of the expansive grounds and halls evoke the ghosts of the ladies who lived, suffered, rejoiced and intrigued between the walls there, Chenonceau is one of the most famous castles in France.*

86 The rooms of the castle are richly decorated, as they must have been at the height of its glory: some good examples are the large kitchen (bottom right), the Gothic gallery with its ogival vaults (left) and the chamber of Gabrielle d'Estrée, King Henri IV's mistress (top right).

86-87 Pure gold and crimson tapestries decorate Louis XIII's chamber, with its magnificent fireplace and the portrait of Louis XIV attributed to Rigaud and set off by a magnificently carved and gilded frame. On the right can be seen the great fireplace with the symbols of the ermine and the salamander, belonging to Francis I and his bride, Claude de France.

87 top The gallery, illuminated by 18 windows ordered by Catherine de Médicis for court banquets, was used as a hospital during the First World War.

88 top The Chambre des Reines is a delightful blend of style and luxury; the room is dominated by Diane de Poitiers' bed, which, according to legend, had an "extraordinary" effect on those who reclined in it.

88 left Italian furniture appeared in French palaces as early as the 16th century. The item shown in this photo, decorated with ivory and mother-of-pearl, is the work of 15th-century Florentine craftsmen.

*89 Diane de
Poitiers' bedroom,
known as the
Chambre des Reines,
contains two
impressive Flemish
tapestries of rare
beauty (the one in the
picture above
portrays scenes from
court life) and a
massive fireplace
decorated with the
royal symbols in pure
gold (right photo).*

*88-89 The chamber
of César de Vendôme,
son of Henri IV and
Gabrielle d'Estrée,
who owned the castle
in the 17th century,
contains a wealth of
gold and tapestries.*

90 The graceful
Renaissance design,
the perfection of the
gallery built by order
of Catherine de
Médicis, the round
feudal keep built at
the corner with the
drawbridge and the
huge grounds, with
Diane's garden on one
side, framed by flower

beds, and Catherine
de Médicis' garden
on the other,
surrounded by great
trees, provided the
setting for the opulent
court life lived on
banks of the Loire
(reconstructed on
summer evenings
today in sound-and-
light shows).

91-94 Chenonceau
Castle, the most
admired and
frequently visited
castle in the Loire
Valley, recounts its
history to 800,000
visitors a year.

95 Chenonceau has inspired generations of painters through the ages; the charm and the tranquil, almost idyllic life of the castle is demonstrated by this 19th-century print, which shows a view of the central building and the bridge connecting it to the keep, with an artist painting the scene below.

CRIME, INTRIGUE AND COURTLY LOVE: BLOIS

"Great souls," wrote Victor Hugo, "have left faint traces of their memory at Blois Castle." Its complex history has given the grandiose construction various styles, from the flowery Gothic of the façade to the Renaissance style of the famous staircase and the classical look of the Gaston d'Orléans wing. In the 14th century this medieval building, designed as a bridgehead on the Loire, belonged to the Counts of Châtillon, the last of whom sold it in 1391 to Duke Louis d'Orléans,

brother of Charles VI. When the duke was killed in Paris by the Burgundian John the Fearless, the castle passed into the hands of Charles d'Orléans, the family poet. Taken prisoner at the battle of Azincourt, Charles was incarcerated for 25 years, comforted by poetry and great literature. When he was released at the end of the Hundred Years' War, Charles d'Orléans thought no more of battle. At the age of 50 he fell in love with the 14-year-old Marie de Clèves, married her and went back to live at Blois Castle, surrounded by writers, artists and an army of architects who demolished the old fortress and erected a stone and brick building.

The complex, with its magnificent Renaissance staircase, was embellished by Francis I, who ascended to the throne in 1515, married Claude de France, by whom he had seven children, and built the famous staircase and the splendid fireplaces. Catherine de Médicis gave an aura of mystery to the royal apartments; behind secret

98 bottom The Renaissance tower and Louis XII wing also overlook the inner courtyard, producing a monumental ensemble of rare beauty. The effect is enhanced by niches like the one shown here. Appearing on the main castle door is this Gothic-style equestrian statue of Louis XII (a 19th-century copy of the original, which was destroyed during the Revolution), decorated by the classic Capetian fleurs-de-lys and a frieze depicting a porcupine.

98-99 Blois reached the height of its power in the 12th and 13th centuries, and continued to play an important role in French political life until the 17th century. In the 18th century, before the Revolution, the town and castle attracted the interest of many French artists. This watercolor, by Henri Joseph Van Blarenberghe, dates from the late 18th century.

doors in her study she concealed precious documents, her famous pearl necklace and, so it was rumored, bottles of poison. Catherine de Médicis' hideaway, which has remained almost intact, still features 237 carved wooden panels that conceal cupboards that can only be opened by pressing a pedal concealed in a plinth. Francis II, Charles IX and Henri III reigned at Blois between 1547 and 1574, directed by their able mother, Catherine de Médicis. The history of the castle recommenced under Henri III. The States General were convened in the huge hall on the ground floor in 1576 to demand the suppression of the Huguenot religion. The States General were again convened in 1588 by Duke Henri de Guise who, supported by the king of Spain, attempted to depose the king. But before going down to the hall where he was expected, Henri III arranged for his rival to be led into a trap and stabbed. The king watched the murder from his chamber. Eight months later, he was to meet the same fate by the hand of Jacques Clément. Until 1617, when Louis XIII sent his mother, Maria de Médicis, into exile there, Blois played no part in history. However, Maria did not stay long. One night, after two years of boredom, she, despite her bulk, climbed down a rope ladder from the window; her son had no choice but to reconcile with his mother after her adventurous escape. However, by then Louis XIII had discovered that Blois, which was quite a long way from Paris, made an excellent gilded prison. In 1626 he sent his brother Gaston d'Orléans there, promising him sufficient funds to build a residence worthy of his rank. Gaston, forgetting his love of political conspiracy, had the architect Mansart draw up plans for a castle, which required the demolition of the existing wings. For three years, work on a new wing opposite the main door in the courtyard proceeded apace. Then, after the birth of Louis XIV, the danger that Gaston might inherit the throne of France receded; Cardinal Richelieu cut off the funds and the work came to a halt. Gaston, dissatisfied with the new section he had built, went to live in the Francis I wing, and devoted his time to collecting rare plants.

99 top left   The influence exerted in France by the discovery of the Italian Renaissance is due to Francis I, who conducted a military campaign in Italy; this influence is particularly evident in the staircase of the Francis I wing in the inner courtyard of Blois Castle.

99 top right   The Gaston d'Orléans wing (the magnificent staircase of which can be seen in this photo) overlooks the inner courtyard. Work on this wing began in 1635 and lasted for three years, until Cardinal Richelieu cut off the funds required.

100 top Visitors can once again follow in the footsteps of Catherine de Médicis at Blois Castle. Her chamber is rich in gold work and luxurious "trifles," such as the four-poster bed and the unusual floor with its gilded tiles framed with the ever-present fleur-de-lys.

100-101 From Catherine's bedroom, access is obtained to her private hideaway, its walls covered with fake panels made of wood and pure gold that conceal secret hiding places.

101 top left and bottom As at Chenonceau, the most luxurious furniture at Blois came from Italy. Tuscan craftsmen, in particular, were very popular in the 15th and 16th centuries, and were particularly respected in France.

101 right Scenes from court life were immortalized by artists of the period, as in this tondo by Ulysse Besnard, known as Ulysse XIX, which shows Catherine de Médicis receiving some ambassadors.

102 top left and bottom The salamander motif, emblem of Francis I, appears in the friezes on the fireplaces and in the furniture made specially for the king.

102 top right This portrait shows Marguerite of Navarre, known as Queen Margot, the sister of King Henri III of France.

102-103 More halls, chambers and galleries of the grandiose Blois Castle, with fireplaces bearing the initials and symbols of Francis I and Claude de France, Renaissance furniture and portraits; the wall decorations, however, are typical of the late 19th and early 20th centuries.

103 top Another 39 historical portraits from the French royal court, as well as Margot's, crowd the gallery in the Louis XII wing.

103 bottom The busts of Henri II, Henri III, Henri IV and Charles IX have been placed in the Galerie des Loges, among magnificent pieces of ivory-inlaid Italian furniture and tapestries of the Flemish school.

104 top The portrait of Louis XIV attributed to Hyacinthe Rigaud pays homage to one of the most powerful French monarchs in history; however, Louis XIV never spent even a day at Blois Castle.

104-105 The rooms, halls and staircases of Blois Castle present the set patterns of what was once the classic style of castle furnishing: the King's Room, with its four-poster bed, the great fireplaces in every room, coffered ceilings and tapestries hanging from the walls.

105 top This picture shows a detail of the tapestry hanging in the bedroom of Henri III; the three fleurs-de-lys, the king's initial and the royal crown are recognizable.

105 bottom The windows illuminating the Salle des États also bear symbols of the Capetian dynasty's power; on the left is the ermine, the emblem of Anne of Brittany, and on the right the porcupine, emblem of Louis XII.

106 and 107 Blois Castle witnessed the ruthless murder of Henri de Guise, treacherously killed by order of King Henri III. The King's Chamber evokes that tragic December 23, 1588, also immortalized in two famous 19th-century canvases.

108 top left The small Beauregard Castle contains a gallery of 327 portraits, unique in the history of the Loire châteaux. The portraits in the long Galerie des Illustres include that of Henry IV on horseback.

108-109 Beauregard Castle, nestled in Russy Forest, is cradled by the calm Beuvron Valley.

THE CHARM OF GREAT MANSIONS: BEAUREGARD AND CHEVERNY

*L*uxuriant, restful countryside leads from Blois to nearby Beauregard Castle, situated at the end of a long drive that cuts through Russy Forest. This small, secluded private castle, its dimensions still as perfect as when it was commissioned in the 16th century by Jean du Thier, secretary of state to Henri II, is worth a visit for its rooms, the large kitchen decorated as in ancient times, and the gallery containing 327 portraits of famous personalities, which is unique in the history of the Loire castles. This Galerie des Illustres was installed by Paul Ardier in the large first-floor gallery that once contained an attractive 16th-century white marble fireplace. The personalities portrayed are prelates, kings, queens, professors and military commanders spanning two centuries. Some pretty delft tiles in the characteristic blue and white colors, laid along the walls in 1628, decorate the austere row of characters hanging side by side, who recount the history of France. At nearby Cheverny Castle, dating from the 17th century, it is the charm of a great mansion, inhabited for 300 years by the family of the marquises of Vibraye and their successor, viscount of Sigelas, that enchants visitors, who can view its magnificent library, painted halls, grandiose weapons room and a collection of 2,000 hunting trophies. The pack of fox-hunting dogs barking excitably from the kennels on one side of the castle recall the great hunting tradition of the castle's owners.

109 top left The 16th-century Cabinet des Grelots is entirely covered with magnificent wood paneling and paintings depicting such subjects as hunting, music and games.

109 top right The great castle kitchen, with its hanging copper pans, is fascinating.

109 bottom right Joan of Arc is portrayed in the Galerie des Illustres.

110-111 The family of the marquises de Vilbraye lived in Cheverny Castle for 300 years. They retained intact the majestic proportions of the rooms, the magnificent furnishings of the king's chamber, as well as the castle's Gobelin tapestries and paintings and valuable prints.

112 top Rooms
containing a wealth
of furnishings and
pure gold lead to the
dining room,
containing a rare
carved cabinet, the
Queen's Room, the
well-stocked library
and the orangery (the
photo shows the gaudy
beamed ceiling).

112-113 Cheverny Castle, made of Bourré stone with slate roofs, is an architectural ensemble with a classical style that marks a development in the evolution of the Loire châteaux.

113 top left The Weapons Room houses part of the castle's extensive collection of military objects.

113 bottom left The large drawing room, in Louis XIII style, contains a wealth of furnishings, from the large red carpet at the foot of the fireplace to the furniture and decorations in blue and pure gold.

113 right The imposing straight Renaissance staircase is flanked by balustrades; the stone it is made of is decorated with reliefs portraying flowers and 18th-century weapons.

A KING'S DREAM: CHAMBORD

*F*inally, we come to Chambord, a mirage from afar and a labyrinth to visit. Visitors should climb the Renaissance staircase, visit the rooms, go out onto the terraces, look down on the huge grounds and come as close as possible to the forest of pinnacles and turrets. This is how the megalomaniac dream of Francis I appears, in all its splendor. That ambitious king, with his ardent temperament and craving for novelty, glory and splendor, concluded his architectural dreams here. Numbers are not everything, but they give some idea of the scale of this magnificent site: 440 rooms, 80 staircases and 365 fireplaces surrounded by about 13,750 acres of perfectly rectangular grounds (about 3,750 of which are open to the public) crowded with deer and wild boar and surrounded by boundary walls about 20 miles long. Chambord is without doubt the most extravagant, exaggerated and majestic castle in the entire Loire Valley. Plundered during the Revolution, belonged then to Marshal Berthier and to the dukes of Bordeaux, then taken over by the government in 1930, Chambord Castle is the unrivaled star of the Loire Valley. Above all it is a hymn to grandeur; with its tufa and slate roof resembling a hanging garden and a thousand pillars, pinnacles, chimney pots and skylights, it would come as no surprise to see fairies or impudent gnomes gamboling there.

*114 and 115
The impressive
Chambord Castle is
the largest in Sologne;
it stands not far from
Blois, and is
surrounded by a huge,
ancient park. Its
construction was
started by order of
Francis I, and
completed during the*

*reign of Louis XIV,
the Sun King. Not
all the rooms in
Chambord Castle are
furnished, but some of
them contain a series
of late 16th-century
Paris tapestries
portraying scenes of
the king's hunt, woven
following cartoons by
Laurent Guyot.*

116-117 The twin
circular staircase,
about 9 yards wide, is
the heart of the great
castle; two people can
go up or down it
without meeting.
The staircase, with
its Renaissance
design, terminates
at the top with a
coffered vault
engraved with a
salamander, the
emblem of Francis I.

117 top left The
rectangular chapel
on the first floor,
situated in a round
tower, is the largest
room in the castle.
It was begun by
Francis I and
finished under Louis
XIV by architect
Harduin-Mansart.

117 top right The
furnishings of
Chambord Castle
are luxurious, and
great attention is
paid to every detail,
as demonstrated by
this radiator covered
with blue and white
majolica in the best
Flemish tradition.

118-119 The Queen's Room, the King's Room and the rooms of the Count of Chambord in Chambord Castle are furnished with valuable furniture, Amiens tapestries, four-poster beds and exquisite carpets.

The luxury exuded by these noble chambers is not reflected in all of the more than 400 rooms in the castle; Francis I's somewhat megalomanic dream of creating the most spectacular, majestic, regal castle in France was brought to an

end by the revolution of 1789, during which Chambord was stripped of much of its finery. However, what remains clearly shows how magnificent it must have been at the height of its glory.

120 Among the most famous portraits at Chambord are those of the castle's founder, Francis I (top left), Henri IV (top right), Louis XIV (bottom left), who stayed there often, and Stanislaw Leczinski, king of Poland and duke of Bar and Lorraine (bottom right).

120-121 The Salle de Compagnie at Chambord Castle contains a magnificent collection of portraits of outstanding personalities from the reigning French monarchy and illustrious foreign guests.

121 bottom
This young face with
an enigmatic smile
belongs to Mlle de
Blois, one of the most
courted and powerful
French women of the
time.

122 top Montigny-le-Gannelon Castle, with its alternating brick and stone decoration and tall slate roofs, dates from the late 14th century, when the defensive structure was beginning to be replaced by the castle residence, still grandiose but more worldly than military.

122-123 High above the Loir River (not to be confused with the Loire), Châteaudun Castle, with its feudal bulk and slate roofs, overlooks the small town below. A stronghold demolished by the Norman Rollon in 911 already existed on the site in the 5th century.

CASTLES AND THE REMEMBRANCE OF THINGS PAST

T o the north of the Loire River, in the romantic heart of France, the great castles become few and far between. Here, the landscape has the fragrance of harvest time, the charm of deserted horizons and, to the west, already heralds the Normandy countryside, with its boundless greenery and pastures. This area contrasts sharply with the grandiose Loire Valley and its magnificent castles, but here, unspoiled nature and wide-open spaces still lead to lesser known castles, that are no less rich in memories and links with the history of the Loire Valley. The castle of Châteaudun is impressive for the steep crag on which it perches, and the castle of Montigny-le-Gannelon for its magnificent furnishings. Another king's mistress, Mme de Maintenon, leads the tour through the splendors of the castle named after her, while Diane de Poitiers lies in Anet Castle, and the dream of grandeur cherished by the marquis de Laborde sleeps at La Ferté-Vidame. Memories of Proust fill the country footpaths and lanes of Illiers-Combray against the distant background of Chartres and its huge cathedral, reaching for the sky.

123 At the end of a narrow street in the village of Illiers-Combray stands the small 19th-century middle-class home of Proust's aunt and uncle, where the famous author spent his Easter holidays as a boy. Everything has remained as it was recounted in À la Recherche du Temps Perdu – the inner garden with its rosebushes and hydrangeas and the author's bedroom are still there.

124-125 *Montigny-le-Gannelon Castle, like nearly all those in the Loire Valley, stands on the remains of an ancient stronghold, this one dating from the 12th century and overlooking the Loir River. The prettier style of the building erected in the 14th century by Jacques de Renty, and frequently altered over the centuries, can be seen from the large entrance park. In 1831 the castle was bought by Prince Montmorency-Laval, who restored the side overlooking the grounds. His son-in-law, the duke of Lévis-Mirepoix, altered the façade overlooking the Loir River in neo-Gothic style and erected a separate building in Baltard style that contains a collection of ancient agricultural machinery.*

MORE HALLS, STAIRCASES AND FORTIFIED WALLS: MONTIGNY-LE-GANNELON AND CHÂTEAUDUN

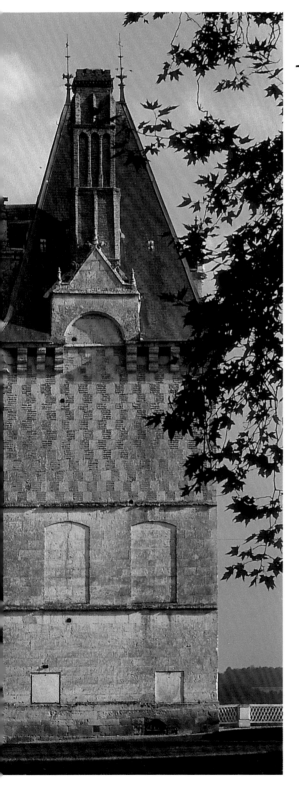

*H*igh above the Loir (not to be mistaken with the Loire), the castle of Montigny-le-Gannelon, already a fortress in the time of Charlemagne, acquired its present name in the year 1000 and its Renaissance style in the 16th century, under Louis XII, when Jacques de Renty demolished the ancient fortress to build a new residence in the contemporary style. All that remains of that project is the Ladies' Tower and the Clock Tower, which were later connected at the base by a Gothic gallery. The property passed through the hands of various owners, statesmen and princes, such as Adrien, lord of Montmorency, duke of Laval and Louis XVIII's ambassador to Rome, Madrid, London and Vienna, who is often mentioned during the visit. This visit is particularly interesting because it is conducted by a member of the present-day family of the viscounts of Talhouët Boisorhand, who live in the castle and know the history and legends of the area. The building was altered on various occasions; the last and most visible alteration was ordered by Count Sigismond de Lévis, who completely rebuilt the east façade overlooking the Loir in 1886.

124 top and 125 right The rooms in the castle, decorated in red, blue and gold, are full of priceless antique furniture and portraits of illustrious members of the family. The castle

now belongs to the descendants of the family of viscount of Talhouët, who personally guide visitors through the castle, recounting its history and mysterious legends.

126 bottom right Three different periods – feudal, Gothic and Renaissance – have given the castle its grandeur. The 12th-century keep is built onto the Sainte-Chapelle, part of the Dunois wing, dating from the 15th century, which is illuminated by large Gothic windows.

The 15 wooden statues in the chapel portray members of the d'Orléans family, carved in the images of saints and beatified personalities, like the tiny Saint Agnes and the Saint Francis, who are none other than Agnès of Savoy and François de Longueville.

Around 6 miles from Montigny-le-Gannelon, the towering bulk of another castle is reflected in the river: this is Châteaudun. The unusual design of the castle, which overlooks the main road to Alençon, is very impressive. However, for visitors arriving from the Chartres direction, the gray walls lose their severe look and acquire the harmony of a Renaissance mansion, with the staircase carved like lace, the great fireplaces, the chapel decorated with magnificent wooden statues, and the tapestries hanging in the reception room.

It was Jean le Dunois who first decided to give his home two faces, representing a compromise between the feudal past and the desire for a more modern residence. The Norman architect Colin du Val, who hailed from Longueville, built the decidedly Renaissance north wing (called the Dunois wing) between the 12th-century tower and the buttress overlooking the Loir. There is a magnificent view from the towers, and as the visit proceeds from room to room the guide tells the stories of Thibault the Trickster, who built the feudal castle (of which nothing now remains), and Jean le Dunois, loyal general of Charles VII and comrade in arms of Joan of Arc at the siege of Orléans, who was the guiding force behind Châteaudun.

128 top In Aunt Léonie's famous room (left) at Illiers-Combray, Proust (portrait on right) was overwhelmed by the memories evoked by a little madeleine dipped into the lime tea served by his aunt.

THE VILLAGE OF THE SWEET MADELEINE

*I*n the huge plain of Beauce, a bell tower pierces the sky like a sharp pencil. "It was the first thing to appear when the train was pulling in to Combray," wrote Proust in *À la Recherche du Temps Perdu.* The pages of his novel seem to turn at every step one takes in the village of Illiers-Combray, which has added the name invented by the author to its own. Here, Proust arrived to spend the Easter holidays at the small house at the bottom of the garden at 4, Rue Docteur-Proust, where many remembrances still remain along with the memory of the sweet, unforgettable madeleine.

Nothing has changed, and on the first floor, Aunt Léonie's room still evokes the atmosphere of that famous page where the author, from the flavor of the morsel of madeleine dipped into the lime tea, recalls past memories. From far off can be seen Chartres Cathedral, which celebrated its 800th anniversary in 1994. At sunset, in the twilit nave, the light sets fire to the reds and blues of the famous 13th-century windows illustrating the lives of the saints, the ancient trades of France, and many Bible stories. The small dark Virgin is venerated at the end of the left-hand aisle. The great statues covering the façade return in the bas-reliefs surrounding the high altar inside, commemorating the art of Jehan de Beauce, who carved the exceptional row of people at prayer in 1514. The still medieval part of the town clusters around the two asymmetrical bell towers in a network of narrow alleys. In the motionless peace of the countryside sleeps Senoches, capital of Perche, the region of good cider. From the small town romantic walks branch off into the nearby forest, around the pond of Lille and La Ferté-Vidame. Nestled in Thymerais Forest, this grandiose patrician residence, now in ruins, still evokes the splendors of the court of the marquis de Laborde, who built his palace in the 18th century on the foundations of the previous castle, where Duke Saint-Simon (author of *Les Mémoires*) lived. The castle was partly destroyed and plundered during the Revolution, and so it has remained until the present day. Fields and meadows protect the abandoned building, which was too large and too magnificent for its bygone splendor to be adequately restored. Maintenon Castle, with its 12th-century keep, the grace of the Renaissance wing and the neoclassical proportions of the side built by Louis XIV, still maintains its royal air. Surrounded by huge grounds, part of which have been sold to the most exclusive golf club in France, the castle was given by Louis XVI to his mistress, Mme de Maintenon, who later became his secret wife. Its drawing rooms and great halls, curtains, velvets, damasks and antique furniture all remain just as they were at the time when the famous lady of the court withdrew with her king to the calm countryside of Eure.

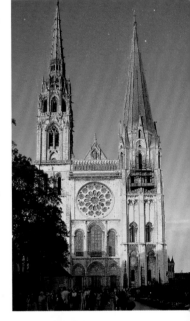

ANET CASTLE: THE TOMB OF BEAUTIFUL DIANE

130 left At the end of the last century the castle was restructured and decorated, and restoration work was carried out on the garden chapel, with its lovely Renaissance dome illuminating an inlaid marble floor that seems to reflect the ornamental motifs of the dome.

From Maintenon it is only a short distance to Anet Castle, the last piece in the huge mosaic of residences associated with the history of the Loire. It was built in 1550 by order of King Henri II, who gave it to his mistress, Diane de Poitiers, as their love nest. The message of this residence is apparent right from the entrance portal, a triumphal arch in honor of "Diana the Huntress," with the naked nymph sculpted by Benvenuto Cellini in the lunette; it was a refuge of pleasure, not a theater of war like many other châteaux of the Loire. The most enlightened minds of the time gathered at Anet, and the king and his mistress went hunting or walked in nearby Dreux Forest. The castle, like many others, was damaged and plundered during the Revolution. It was sold, the furniture was scattered, and part of the castle was demolished by unscrupulous purchasers. In 1820 it was bought by the duchess of Orléans and restored for the first time. However, it was to take years, until nearly the end of the century, before M. Moreau and his descendants restored the home so that it was worthy of the history it recounts. Now preciously decorated, each room evokes the memory of the king's lovely mistress. Four tapestries woven especially for her in 1552 decorate the Salle des Gardes; other Flemish tapestries drape the walls of the room containing a fireplace decorated with an alabaster medallion by Jean Goujon; the four-poster bed with its canopy bears her initials and sentimental souvenirs belonging to Diane are displayed in the Red Room. In the courtyard is the entrance to Saint Thomas' Chapel. Diane's tomb is in the garden, behind the chapel. After the king's death, she took lonely refuge in this castle, where she lived until her death in 1566. Her last residence closes the romantic and dissolute history of the Loire Valley castles.

130 top and 130-131
Anet Castle was King
Henri II's gift to his
lovely mistress, Diane
de Poitiers. Here the
king and Diane
retreated for short
periods, far from the
splendors and court
intrigue characteristic
of the castles closest to
the Loire. The
residence, situated on
the edge of Dreux
Forest, is a gem of
secluded Renaissance
beauty.

130 bottom right
Diane de Poitiers
(portrayed here as
Diana the Huntress)
retired to Anet after
the death of King
Henri II, when
Catherine de Médicis
took revenge by
confiscating
Chenonceau Castle.

131 The spirit of the
beautiful Diane can be
felt in every corner of
the castle, from the
splendid main staircase
(top left) to the
bedroom, with its
decorations, tapestries,
paintings and four-
poster bed (top right),
to the Salle des Gardes
(center right), decorated
with huge Fontainebleau
tapestries, to the
exquisite wood-paneled
Red Room (bottom
right).

136 Bouges Castle,
built in the 18th
century, is situated
at the border between
the forests to the north
of Valençay and the
plains to the south of
Châteauroux. The
gardens of Bouges-le-
Château follow
Italian patterns,
with classical designs
and decorations (such
as the hedge cut to a
fleur-de-lys shape
shown in the photo).

INDEX

MUSEUM AND ART COLLECTIONS